ZONAL DEFENDING

THE FLAT BACK FOUR...
AND ALL THAT STUFF!

A guide for coaches, players and referees

by Jack Detchon

First published June 30th, 1996 by WORLD OF SOCCER
5880 Falcon Road, West Vancouver, British Columbia
(800) 762-2378

ISBN 1-896466-11-7

Second printing February 1999

796.334
D48

CREDITS:
Editor: Bob Dunn
Graphics: Lincoln Dunn
Layout and Design: Dunn Communications
Technical Editor: Tony Waiters

Manufactured by Hemlock Printers Ltd.

ACKNOWLEDGEMENT

To Allen Wade, my former boss, still my mentor and a
good friend.

DEDICATION

To my wife Vicky, who has constantly supported me, and has long wanted me to "put pen to paper."

Also to our two daughters, Nancy and Laura, who still believe that "Dad can do anything."

TABLE OF CONTENTS

INTRODUCTION

WHY THIS BOOK WILL HELP SOCCER IN NORTH AMERICA

by Tony Waiters, Technical Editor

In the early part of 1995, Jack Detchon and I were fellow staff instructors on an National Soccer Coaches Association of America (NSCAA) Advanced National Academy at Boca Raton. Craig Brown, the Scottish national coach, was the guest clinician. As usual, he put on a very interesting yet thought-provoking session — including a summary of the zonal system used by Brazil in winning the World Cup at USA '94.

Zonal Defending was the hot topic of the week. What is it? How does it work? What are the advantages and disadvantages? Is there only one form of Zonal Defending? How do you introduce it to players brought up on a man-marking system? How do you teach zonal play? Is Zonal Defending better than man marking? The discussions went on. On the field. Off the field. At happy hour...often long into the night.

By the end of the week, I'm delighted to report that I had persuaded Jack to do this manual. And so provide some, if not all, of the answers.

I'm going to provide one answer before Jack even gets a start!

There is no one "best" system of play. As Allan Brown, the old Sheffield Wednesday and Sunderland coach, would say: "There are many ways up Everest."

However, if your players understand how to play effectively in a man-marking/sweeper system AND understand how to play in a zonal system, they will be better players.

So this is Jack Detchon's book, and he has done an excellent job. It's simple, clear and spot on.

To the body of Jack's work, both he and I have added a little "color" — so we don't get too serious about this great and fun game, soccer.

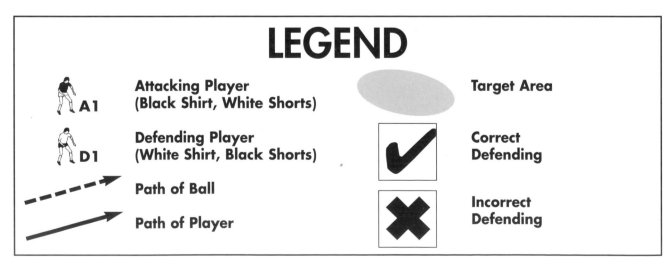

LEGEND

A1 — Attacking Player (Black Shirt, White Shorts)

D1 — Defending Player (White Shirt, Black Shorts)

Path of Ball

Path of Player

Target Area

✔ Correct Defending

✖ Incorrect Defending

CHAPTER ONE

Man-for-Man or Zone?

It is understandable why many, if not most, American soccer teams — whether they be male or female, children or adult — tend to play with a sweeper behind two, three or four close markers.

The marker knows his job — "Mark number nine!" — almost to the detriment of everything else. The sweeper's job is basically to offer cover between the opponent with the ball and the goal, or between the ball and the goal. The degree of cover, i.e. the distance between the marker and the sweeper, depends largely on the distance the play is from the defenders' goal.

This way of defending, therefore, offers a simplicity that's equally attractive to both the coach and the players.

The system does, however, have major drawbacks:

1) It offers space behind the markers for the attacking team to exploit without the danger of going offside. In Diagram 1, **A8** is able to receive the ball in the shaded space behind **D3** and **D2** to make it a 1 vs 1 with sweeper **D5**.

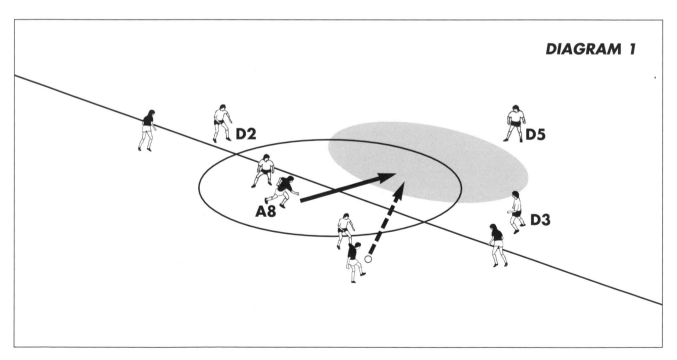

DIAGRAM 1

Drawbacks of the sweeper behind the markers.

2) An attacking player who is marked man to man can easily move the marker and create space for the attacking team to exploit — Diagrams 2 & 3

In Diagrams 2 & 3, attacker **A7** makes a 15-yard inside run and creates the space shown by the shaded area for **A2** to run into and receive the ball.

If sweeper **D5** now steps up to challenge **A2**, the defense has no cover.

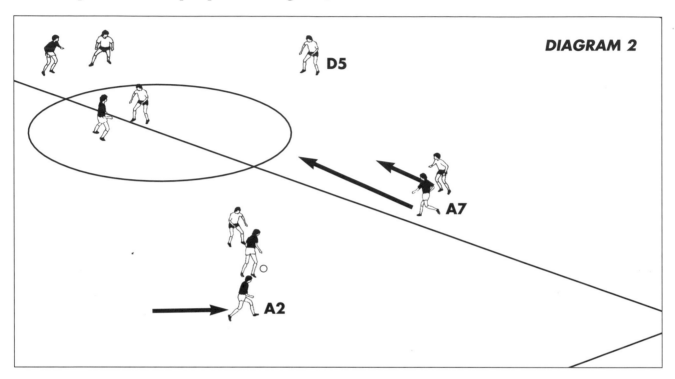

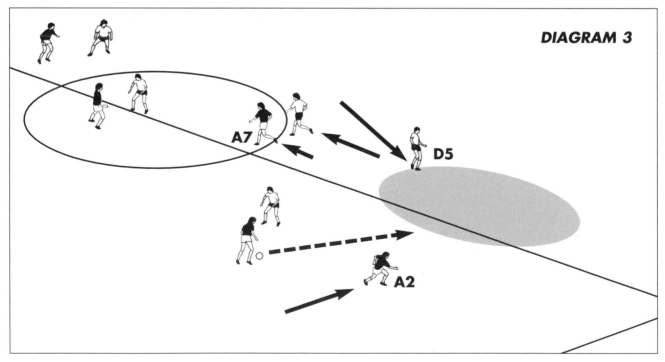

Diagrams 2 & 3 — Drawbacks of the sweeper/man-marking system

A — Attacking Player   D — Defending Player

Both these major drawbacks can be overcome by a space-marking — as opposed to a man-marking — back line. Compare Diagram 4 to Diagram 1.

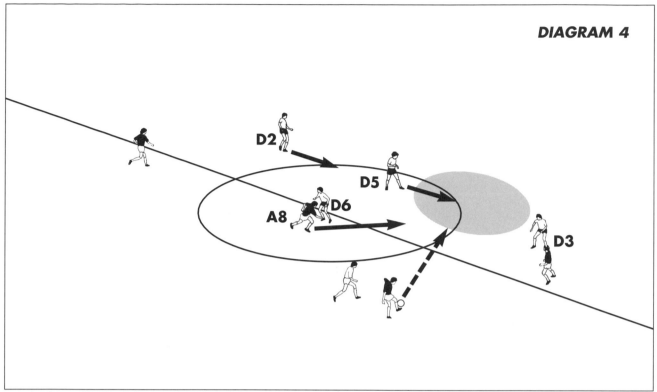

DIAGRAM 4

Employing a flat-back line with zonal defending.

In Diagram 4, if **A8** tries to attack the space behind **D3**, **D6**'s marking position — compared with the tight man-to-man position — makes the run difficult. If **A8** gets away from **D6**, **D5** picks up **A8** and **D6** takes over **D5**'s position. Even if **D6** falls in a challenge, **D5** can pick up **A8** and **D2** can provide cover.

Lastly, if **A8**'s run is naive — i.e. too early and or too straight — both **D3** and **D5** can let **A8** run "offside" (see "We don't play offside" in the appendix).

TIPS FOR DEFENDERS

1. *Do not assume because a striker or forward outwardly appear so disinterested that they no longer care. In a flash, they can switch on and score.*

2. *Do not assume the ball is going to roll out of play. Wind, longer grass or mud may stop it. Forward players who pursue "lost causes"*

sometimes benefit in these circumstances. Take nothing for granted.

3. *Do not go to ground to slide tackle unless you are 100% sure you will get the ball, or unless there is no other way left open to you. A player on his backside makes trouble for his own side.*

A — Attacking Player   D — Defending Player

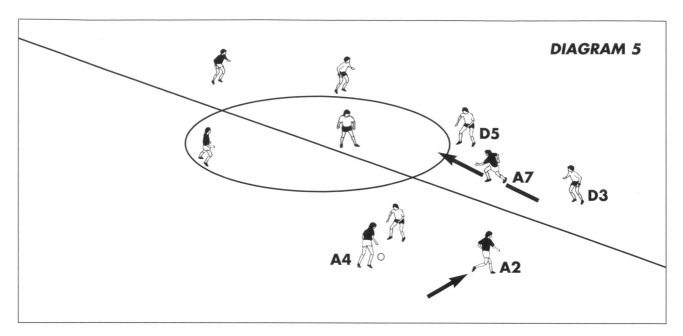

DIAGRAM 5

Passing players on.

In Diagram 5, if **A4** has the ball, the distribution of the zonal marking or Back Four players is slightly different to the sweeper marking in Diagram 2. Therefore, when **A7** makes the diagonal run IN FRONT of **D5**, **D5** picks up **A7** as **D3** is prepared to pass the player on. **D3** then maintains position in that zone, marks the important space and either deters or confronts **A2** — Diagram 6.

The so-called "flat" Back Four is not flat for most of the game, as will be shown later. But it does "push up" or "step." This has the effect of constricting the midfield and shortening the playing area, thus making play more difficult for the attacking side.

The sweeper system tends to lengthen the playing area and therefore gives more space to the attacking team to pass or run the ball.

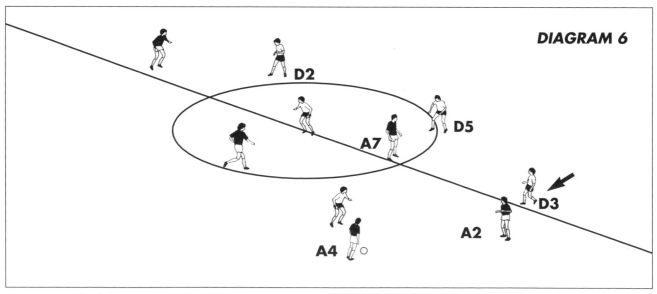

DIAGRAM 6

Pressure on the ball determines backline positions.

A — Attacking Player   D — Defending Player

With **A4** unpressurized in Diagram 6, the back line holds its ground. When **D6** closes down on **A4**, the back line can "push up" and force the attackers back toward their own half, constricting the space in which they are able to play (see Diagram 6A).

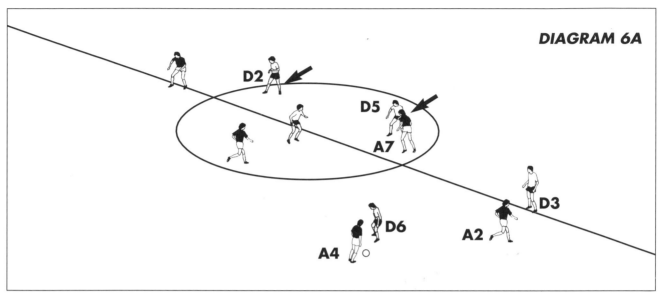

DIAGRAM 6A

Backline pushes up as a result of pressure on the ball.

More Tips for Defenders

1. If an attacker you are marking "comes off you" and goes toward his own goal, follow him until you can pass him on to a midfield player. If he goes sideways, you can usually pass him on. If he goes diagonally behind the Back Four, track him or let him run offside. Be on your toes mentally and physically.

2. Never listen to what your opponents say, whether it is complimentary or otherwise. Remember the world is full of trickery and attacking players are as tricky as a cart load of monkeys.

3. Keep a mental (or for that matter a written) record of opponents' tricks, fouls and tendencies, e.g., Player A likes to beat you with his first touch, Player B rarely if ever goes left, Player C never shoots with his left foot. Forewarned is forearmed!

4. Although we all like to play controlled soccer, never be afraid to clear the ball high wide and long. Nobody can score when the ball is 30 feet in the air.

5. Decide early and, if necessary, make your mistake early. Perhaps there will be time to rectify it. A late wrong decision can be fatal.

A — Attacking Player   D — Defending Player

Shouting for SHOOTING

It is possible, though unlikely, for the Ford Motor Company to manufacture a car without any members of the workforce talking to each other. However, the frustration would be considerable and it would take a long time. If defenders become frustrated with each other, don't communicate and take a long time to do things, the team will lose games in the same way that Ford would lose money.

Playing soccer is no different from any other human co-operative venture, whether it is making a car, building a home or conducting open heart surgery. The need to let people know what you are doing, for them to let you know what they want you to do, and for all the people concerned to do one thing, etc., all improve with good verbal communication.

Good forward players and midfield players are tricky, crafty customers and the more eyes that watch them the better. In order for the Back Four or Back Three to be at its best, constant talking between each player and the goalkeeper is vital. The goalkeeper is also the Back Four's sweeper and is VITAL in this communication network. The keeper is in the best position to see the big picture.

All five players need to speak the same language and use the same vocabulary, e.g., "force him out" means make the attacker go right (or left). "Push up" means go forward as a unit, stop and then step back when/if the opposition gains possession.

The way of speaking or shouting to each other needs to be urgent but composed and, above all, sensible and intelligent. I know a goalkeeper who as a corner kicker approaches to kick the ball from the left with his right foot always shouts "inswinger". But it's obvious the corner will be an inswinger, so that communication is unnecessary. Such chatter can become like background music or the message from the boy who cried wolf! Ignored. Players do not have time to be selective in their advice taking, therefore ALL advice needs to be IMPORTANT.

Good shouting/talking is vital to good defensive play and should be taught and encouraged at the earliest possible age.

CHAPTER TWO

Defining the Zones

It is remarkable that teams as diverse as Brazil and Ireland, Inter Milan and Manchester United, Italy and Norway, USA, Sweden and Switzerland play with a Back Four.

Maybe six of the above soccer nations are relatively recent converts to this way of defending, but they have all been, to a degree, successful in employing this method of defending.

The basic tenent of space/zone marking is that the nearer the ball — or the player with the ball — is to the player in your space, the closer you are required to mark him.

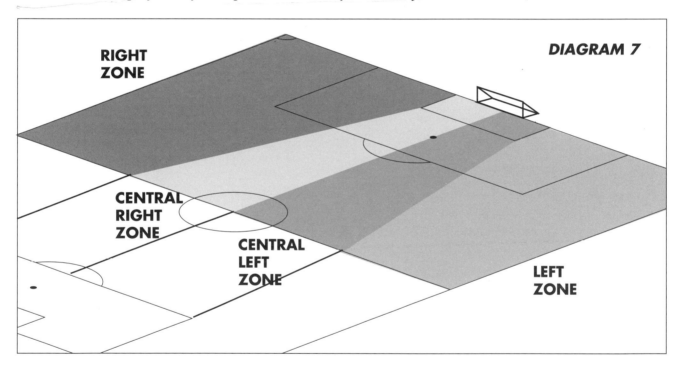

RIGHT ZONE

CENTRAL RIGHT ZONE

CENTRAL LEFT ZONE

LEFT ZONE

DIAGRAM 7

Using a traditional Back Four philosophy, the defending half of the field has been divided into four zones (Diagram 7). The central zones (left and right), while smaller than the left and right zones, are the most critical.

A — Attacking Player   D — Defending Player

In Diagram 7a, **D2** & **D3** will tend to play most of the game in their zones. They will also spend time in their nearest adjacent central zone — particularly when play is on the other side of the field.

Defenders **D5** & **D6** will tend to play mainly in the two central zones but they will spend some time in their nearest right and left zones, respectively, as they support or cover the outside defender or maybe track a diagonal run.

These positional rules of thumb may be disregarded at free kicks and corner kicks.

Each defender is responsible for the opponent who comes into that defender's zone. If more than one player enters that zone, then that zonal defender must ensure that either:

a) a Back Four player picks up the attacker (and the other two slide over), or
b) a midfield player does the job by dropping back.

Rarely, if ever, will both **D5** & **D6** be outside the central zones at the same time.

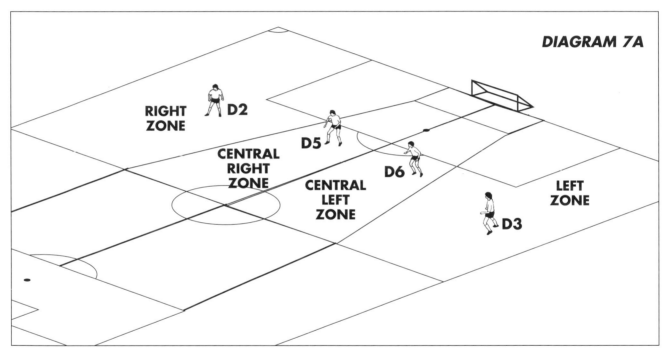

The movement between zones for the back players.

• •

'Trust Your Head!' — Charlton

Jack Charlton, who will be remembered more now for being the manager/coach of Ireland, was a formidable center back both for England in winning the 1966 World Cup and for Leeds United in the English First Division.

When talking about high crosses into the box, Jack said that a center back should always head those balls he could, and NEVER leave the ball to a goalkeeper or other defenders despite their maybe having called him to leave it. Said Jack:

"TRUST NOBODY!"

A — Attacking Player   D — Defending Player

CHAPTER THREE

Defenders' Responsibilities — Marking

1 vs 1

Defenders must always keep in mind that their jobs are to win back the ball and attack the opposition. However, it will not always be possible for defenders to do this because the opposition, by good "first touch" and subsequent good control or rapid one-touch passing, will not allow it. It is then that the defender(s) must be alert, vigilant and switched-on, yet patient.

In Diagram 8, in a grid area 10 yards by 30 yards, the server passes the ball to **A1**, who tries to turn and play the ball to the **Target Player.** The defender is **D2**. The coach can condition the starting positions of **A1** and **D2** to vary the situations.

DIAGRAM 8

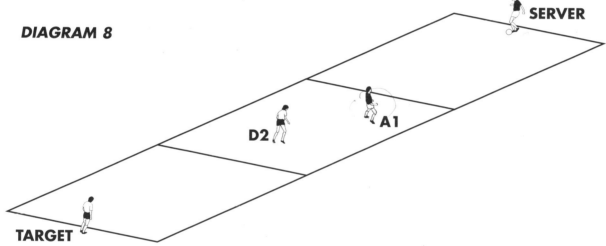

KEY FACTORS

- While the ball is travelling, cover the distance to marking position as fast as possible but under control.

- Adopt a slightly-crouched and sideways position within touching distance of the attacking player.

- Be patient.

- Do not allow the attacker to turn by:
    - a) close physical proximity,
    - b) threatening the ball.

- Also, if the defender fails to close down, the attacker is allowed to: (a) stay "heads up" and see the big picture and (b) play a penetrating pass past or over the defender.

A — Attacking Player   D — Defending Player

Remember that being too close is as dangerous as not being close enough. If the defender is too close the attacker will turn, using the defender's body. If the defender is too far away, the attacker will turn and confront the defender. The ideal distance is to be where the defender can, if desired, reach forward and just touch the attacker with the hand that is nearest.

In Diagrams 9 and 10, **A1** and **D2** are positioned in such a way that **A1** has time to turn when receiving the ball and, if **D2** does not defend skillfully, **A1** will play the ball to the **Target Player.**

DIAGRAM 9

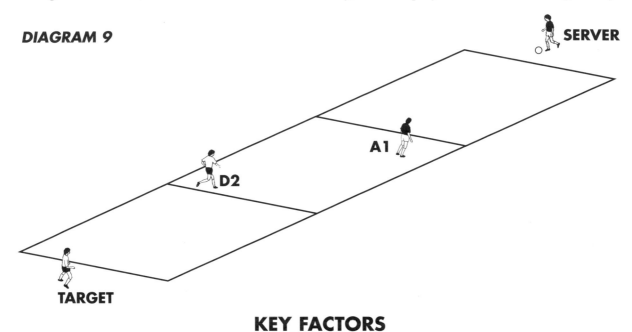

KEY FACTORS

- Approach in such a way that you get into the intended line of pass and, at the same time, close down **A1**.
- Adopt good, low defending position, almost half-turned.
- Threaten the ball.
- Be patient.

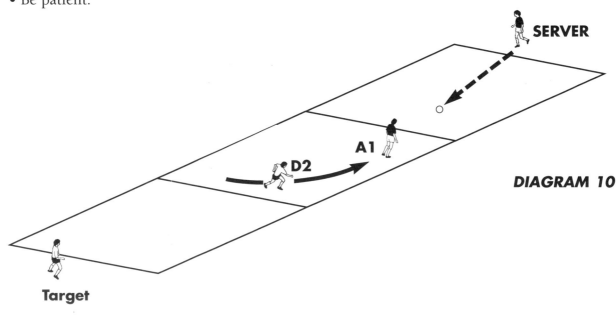

A — Attacking Player   D — Defending Player

CHAPTER FOUR

Defenders' Responsibilities — Marking and Covering

DEFENDING 2 vs 2

This is the simplest situation when a defender is faced with the question: "Do I mark the player, or do I mark the space?"

In Diagram 11, the **Server** at the end line plays the ball to **A2** and **A3**, who will try to pass the ball to the **Target**. Defending are **D4** and **D5**.

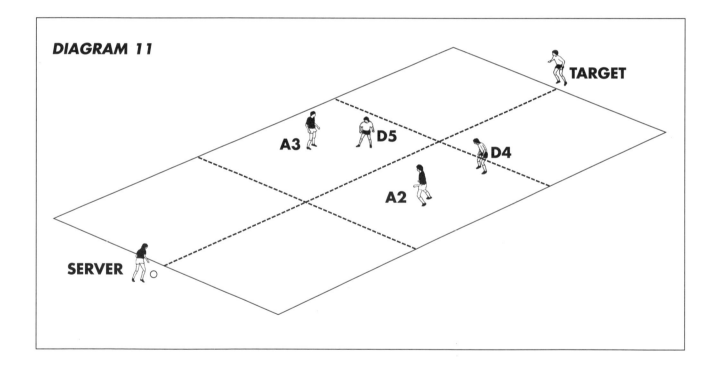

DIAGRAM 11

The grid area is 30 yards by 20 yards.

If the coach so desires, the practice can be reversed so that, at the end of the sequence, the **Target** becomes the **Server** and the roles of the players within the grid can be changed from attacker to defender, and vice-versa.

Please Note: In all illustrations and practices in this and the following chapters, the offside law applies.

A — Attacking Player   D — Defending Player

In Diagram 12, the **Server** passes the ball to **A3**, in **D5**'s zone. So it is **D5**'s responsibility to mark **A3** closely. In fact, **D5** should have moved into this position as the ball travels. **D4**'s job is now to cover for **D5** and encourage **A3** to pass in front of **D5** and **D4** rather than attack the space behind **D5**.

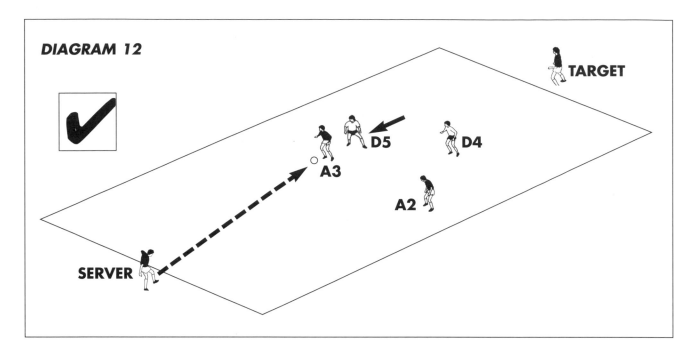

DIAGRAM 12

TARGET
D5
D4
A3
A2
SERVER

KEY FACTORS

For **D5**, it is the same as individual 1-vs-1 defending:

• Cover the distance to a touch-tight position as the ball travels to **A3**.

• Body position crouched and half-turned.

• Don't let player turn.

• Be patient.

For **D4**, positioning depends upon two factors.

• Angle — **D4** must be at such an angle that:

    a) **D4** can cover **D5**.

    b) **D4** can mark **A2** if the ball is switched.

• Distance — close enough to **D5** so as to deal with **A3** if **A3** were to beat **D5** but not so close that **A3** can beat both players with one touch.

A — Attacking Player   **D — Defending Player**

If **A3** switches the ball to **A2** (Diagram 13), **D4** becomes the marker and **D5** the support or covering player, guarding the valuable space behind **D4**.

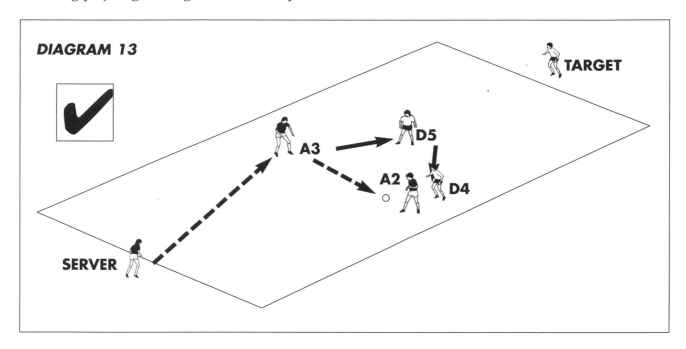

If **D5** does not move and give cover to **D4** when the ball is switched (Diagram 14), **A2** and **D4** are in a 1-vs-1 situation, which is good attacking odds. **A2** can now attack **D4**. **D5** is encouraging **A2** to do this. But in Diagram 13, the excellent position of **D5** is encouraging **A2** to play across **D4** and **D5** back to **A3**. This is good defending.

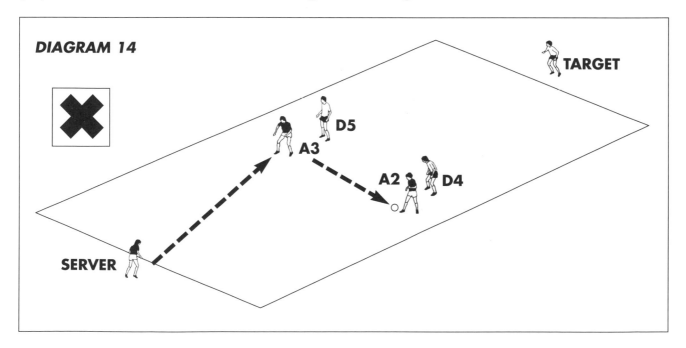

Thus, you see players learning that good Zonal Defending denies good attacking possibilities and encourages less penetrative possibilities.

A — Attacking Player   D — Defending Player

In Diagram 15, **D4's** support position is too flat.

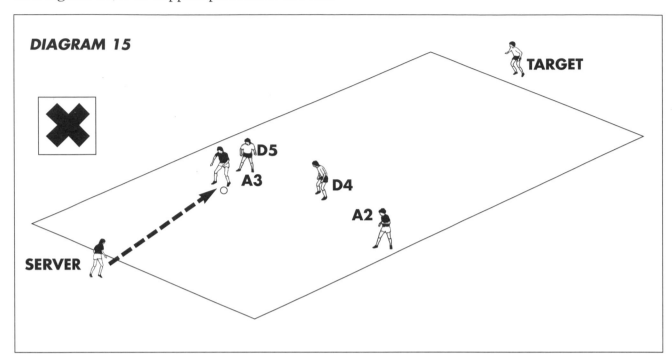

In Diagram 16, **D4's** support position is too steep.

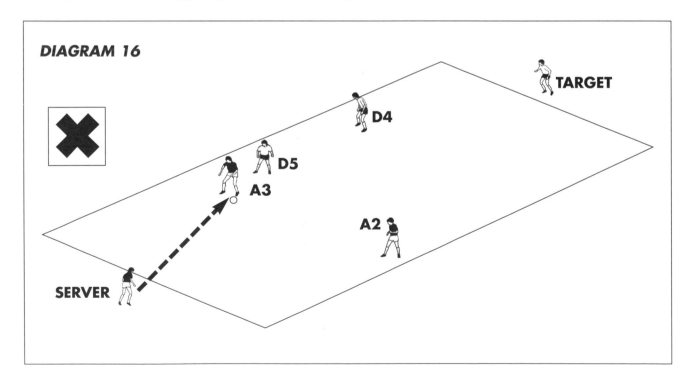

A — Attacking Player   D — Defending Player

In Diagram 17, **D4's** support position is too close.

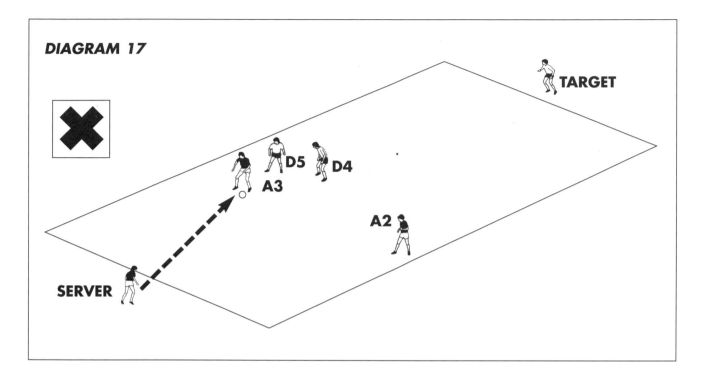

In Diagram 18, **D4's** support position is too distant.

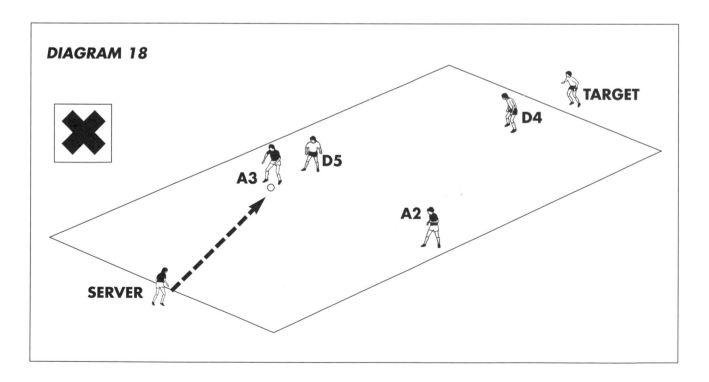

In Diagram 19, **D4** is in exactly the right position:

a) **D4** can cover and help **D5**.

b) If the ball is switched, **D4** is close enough to mark **A2**.

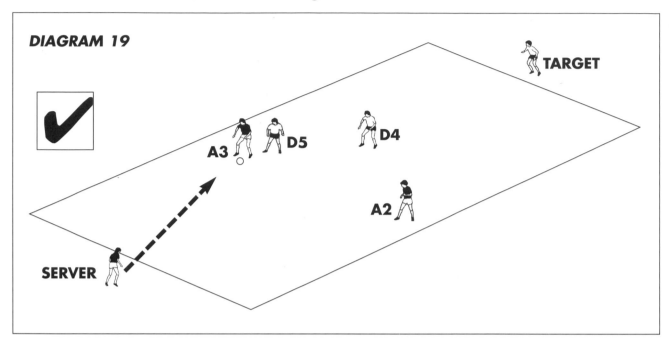

DIAGRAM 19

Putting On the Cover

As the manager/coach of Plymouth Argyle in the mid-'70s, I employed a zonal system. Nothing too different about that. Most English teams played it that way. They still do today. But we were having some difficulty with the Back Four, particularly when play was switched.

The players were slow in responding to the changing circumstances and not sliding inside from the now weak side. So we spent the bulk of the tactical preparation one week on this problem as we prepared for an important on-the-road title game.

On the Saturday, riding in the team bus to the game, as we turned a corner the toolbox in the trunk of the bus scraped and screeched its way from one side of the trunk to the other.

"What's that?" I shouted.

"Sounds like our Back Four putting the cover on," replied Bobby Saxton, center-back and team comedian.

— Tony Waiters

A — Attacking Player   D — Defending Player

These angles and distances can be illustrated even better if the attacking players are facing the defenders with the ball (Diagram 20).

If **D4**'s angle is too steep, that encourages **A3** to play the ball past **D5** and **D4** so that **A2** can run onto the ball.

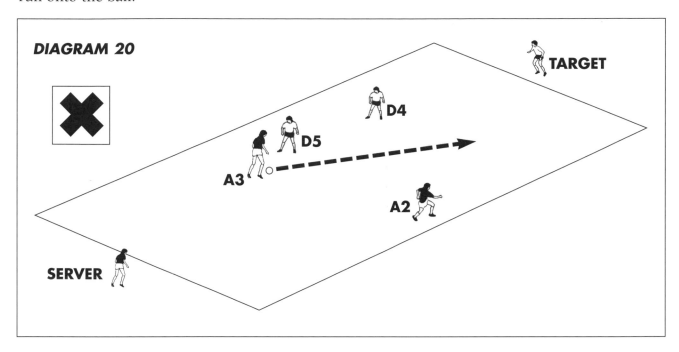

If **D4**'s distance is too great, it produces a 1-vs-1 situation between **A3** and **D5**. Or, if A3 plays forward and behind **D5**, it becomes **A2** vs **D4** (Diagram 20A).

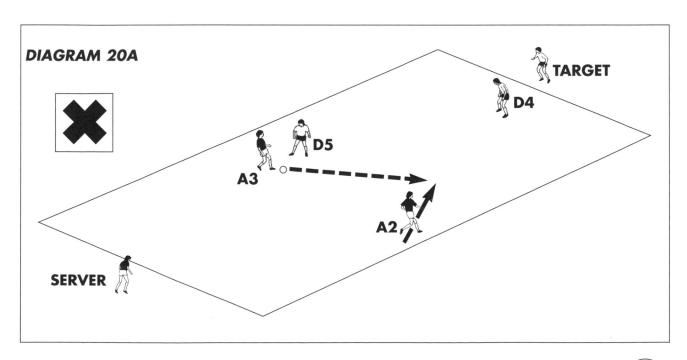

A — Attacking Player   D — Defending Player

If **D4** takes up the correct angle (Diagram 21), that pass is discouraged, or it will likely be intercepted.

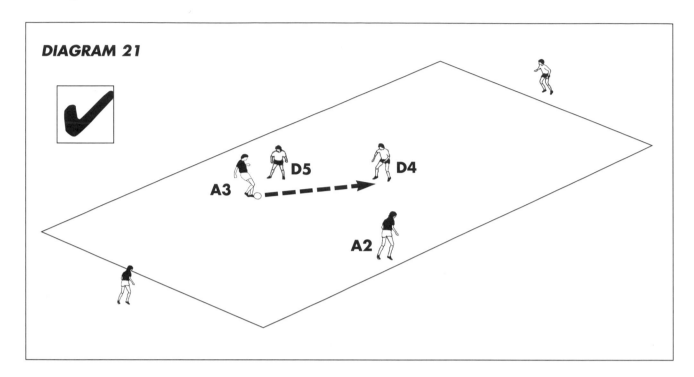

DIAGRAM 21

Good defenders MUST NOT be ball watchers. They have to be game watchers. In Diagram 21, D4 needs to observe the other three players (two attackers and one teammate) and the ball. Ball watchers tend to be ball followers — if only for a short time. Take the situation in Diagram 22.

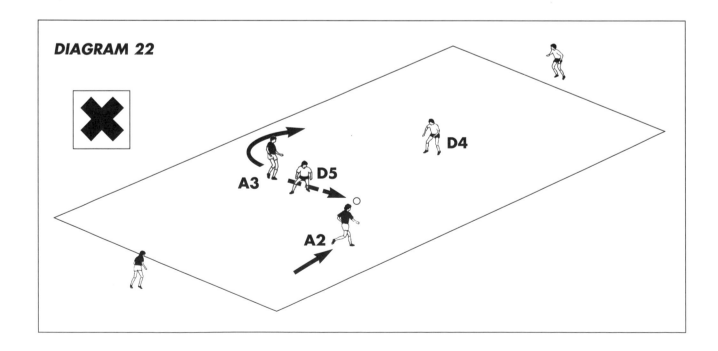

DIAGRAM 22

A — Attacking Player   D — Defending Player

A3 has the ball and plays to A2. If D5 watches only the ball and moves toward it by only half a stride, D5 is wide open to being beaten by a wall pass or a one-two (Diagram 23).

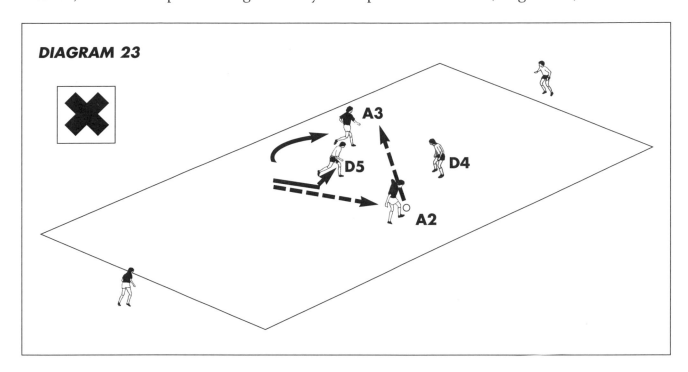

DIAGRAM 23

What D5 must do, as the ball is transferred to A2, is move backwards and slightly sideways into that covering position which denies the through pass (Diagram 24).

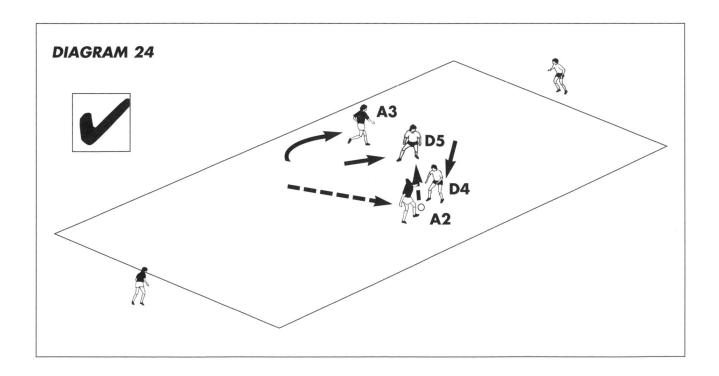

DIAGRAM 24

A — Attacking Player   D — Defending Player

CHAPTER FIVE

Defenders' Responsibilities — Marking, Covering and Balancing

3 VS 3

As defending 2 vs 2 is more difficult than defending 1 vs 1 because of the expanded parameter of understanding, so is 3 vs 3 more difficult than 2 vs 2.

In the previous chapter, the following key factors have been established:

1) Near defender goes tight to pressure. Defender's position is slightly crouched, half-turned and within touching distance of the attacker. Having reached that position while being aware of the possibility of winning the ball, defender must be patient and responsible.

2) The second defender's job is to cover or support the first pressuring player. The second defender's position will be determined: a) by the angle of support and b) by the distance of support.

Advancing into defending 3 v 3, you will find that the third defender's job is to balance the defense and deny the attacking team good targets or attacking possibilities.

In Diagram 25, using an area approximately 40x30 yds, **A2** is the nearest attacker to **A1**, who has the ball. **D2** is therefore marking closer than any other defender. As the ball travels to **A2**, **D2** marks closer. **D3** gives cover in the dangerous space behind **D2**. **D4** occupies the dangerous space behind **A3**. Since **A4** is the farthest attacker from **A1**, **D4** can mark furthest away.

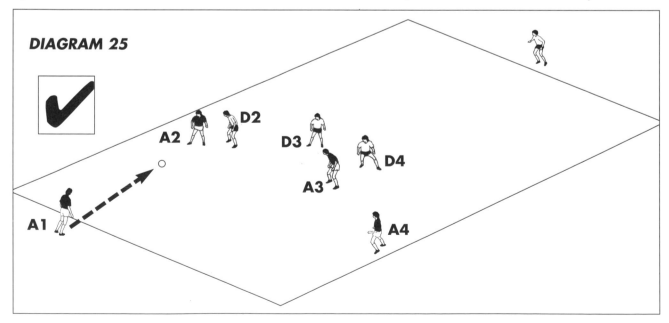

DIAGRAM 25

A — Attacking Player   D — Defending Player

If **A1** changes his mind and plays the ball to **A4** (Diagram 26), the position changes.

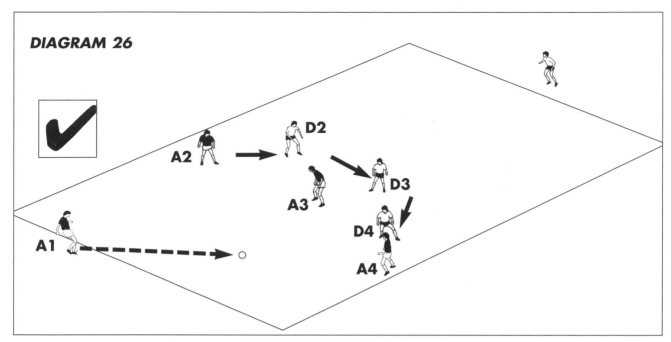

DIAGRAM 26

As **A1** turns, manipulates the ball and passes it, **D4** makes a quick assessment: "Can I intercept?" or "Can I tackle?" If the answer to both these questions is "No!" then **D4** takes up a touch-tight marking position. **D3** moves from one side of **A3** to the other, to cover for **D4**. **D2** moves into the balancing position. This now encourages **A4** to play the ball either back or across the field.

Consider the position if **D2** does not balance — particularly if **A4** happens to turn with the ball (Diagram 27). **A4** is now being encouraged to play the ball behind the defense and into the shaded area.

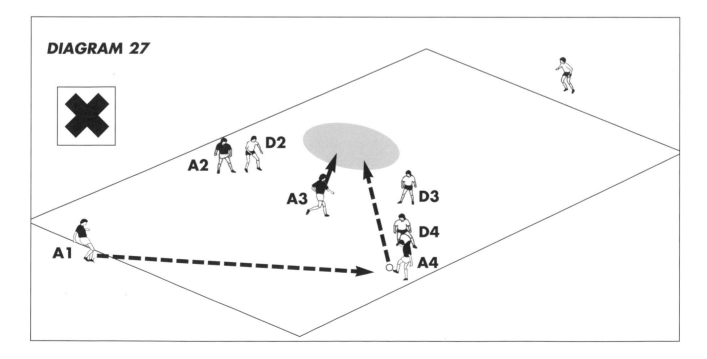

DIAGRAM 27

A — Attacking Player   D — Defending Player

If **D3** takes responsibility for that wider area (Diagram 28), this only complicates the defensive problem, encouraging **A4** to play through the central area toward the goal or, in this instance, the Target Player, **A3**.

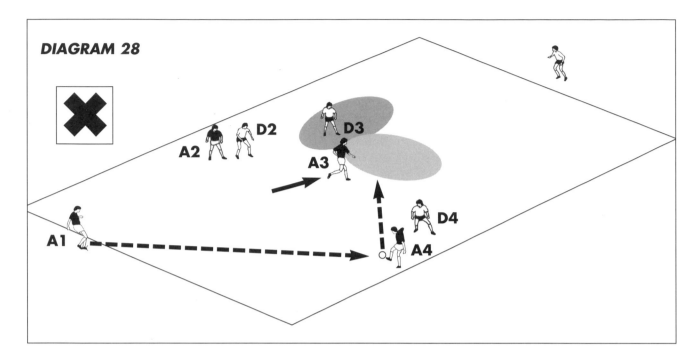

DIAGRAM 28

Soccer's classic case of the 'shorts!'

Fashions change, social mores change and soccer changes.

Thirty years ago, I was playing senior semi-pro soccer in England — in the newly-invented Back Four, of course! After a tackle my opposing winger had his shorts badly torn.

It was a perfectly fair challenge — as I recall!

Today, he would simply remove them and put on a new pair. However, in the yet-to-be-named "swinging" '60s, there was a different code of behavior.

Players would all gather around the

"shortless player" so that the females in the crowd would be spared the sight of his nether regions.

As this procedure was taking place, the crowd of 3000-plus had gone very quiet when from a group of several women came the dulcet female shout:

"Michael, would you like to borrow a pair of mine?"

There was a slight pause and Michael, who incidentally was a barrister, shouted back:

"No thank you, Madam! Canvas tends to chafe me!!"

A — Attacking Player   D — Defending Player

CHAPTER SIX

The Complete Back Four

Zonal Defending is defending in such a way that you offer the attacking players areas to attack which good attackers would not normally take and deny them access to areas they would very much prefer.

All defenses tend to concentrate in the center of their penalty area and deny attackers the chance to shoot at goal from central positions. They prefer to deflect shooting chances wide of, say, the line of the 6-yard box (Diagram 29).

The defenders will try to stop **A6**, **A8** & **A9** from shooting, but may be prepared to allow **A11** and **A10** to shoot from wider and further away.

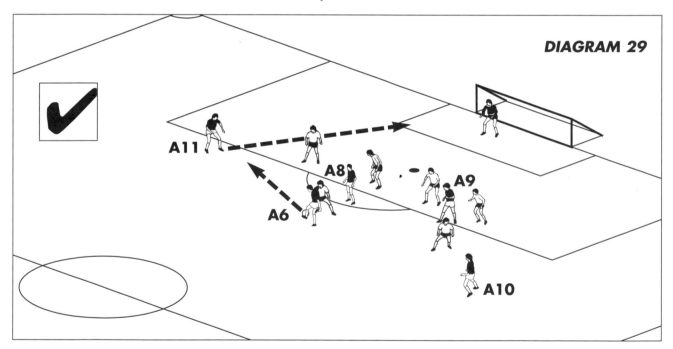

DIAGRAM 29

Similarly, Zonal Defending hopes to encourage attackers to play in front of defenders rather than behind and, if they do play behind the defenders, the defenders (including the goalkeeper) will be first to the ball.

A — Attacking Player   D — Defending Player

Probably the simplest way to present Zonal Defending is to study players' duties or jobs:

First Defender's Job

This is the player who is: a) nearest the ball or
b) marking the player nearest to the ball or
c) confronting the player with the ball

The First Defender's job is to pressure, stop the ball from being played forward, encourage square or back passes and, of course, to win the ball if possible.

Second Defender's Job

This is usually the nearest player to the pressurizing defender, whose job it is to cover or support the First Defender, both physically and verbally.

Third Defender's Job

This defender's job is to balance the defense by occupying vital or dangerous space. On occasion, there may be more than one "Third Defender."

If you now look at a complete Back Four, you can now examine their marking positions vis-a-vis their jobs, i.e., First Defender, Second Defender, Third Defender. Although nowadays you rarely see four forwards employed as a front four, that opposition format will be used to clarify how Zonal Defending can cope with that degree of attack.

KEY FACTORS IN COLLECTIVE DEFENDING

- The defense should be goalside.

- The defender should be between attacker and goal. Defending "in to out" (Diagram 30).

- The defender's distance from the attacker should be that distance which the defenders can cover while the ball is travelling to another attacker. This is approximately 1/3 of the length of the pass.

In Diagram 30, each defender is: (a) goalside of his attacker, (b) between the attacker and the goal and (c) with a marking distance that is different from the other defenders since they are all different distances from the ball.

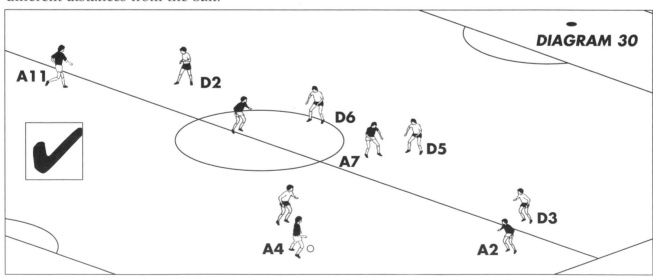

Distances and marking position of the Back Four.

A — Attacking Player   D — Defending Player

So **D3** is close because **A2** is near the ball, and **D2** is the furthest away to balance the defense, because **A11** is furthest away from the ball — perhaps 40 to 45 yards.

In Diagram 30, if **A8** decides to switch the play, the pass will probably be to the feet of **A11**, since **D2** occupies the space in front of **A11**. However, If **D2** doesn't take up this balancing position and instead marks **A11** closely (Diagram 31), **D2** is encouraging **A8** to play the ball over and behind the defense into what, for the defenders, is dangerous space.

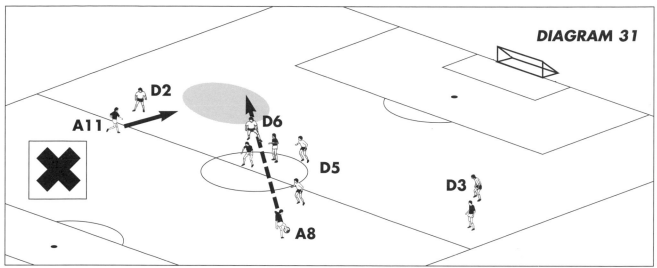

Lack of balance leaves dangerous space.

If **D2** maintains balancing position, **A8** — in switching the play — will play to **A11**'s feet. As the ball is moving between **A8** and **A11**, **D2** must cover the distance to **A11** and decide:

• Can **D2** intercept the pass?
• Can **D2** tackle **A11** as **A11** receives the ball?
• Does **D2** pressure **A11** (**A11** having received the ball)?

D6, **D5** and **D3** change their positions — again as the ball is in transition from **A8** to **A11** (Diagram 32).

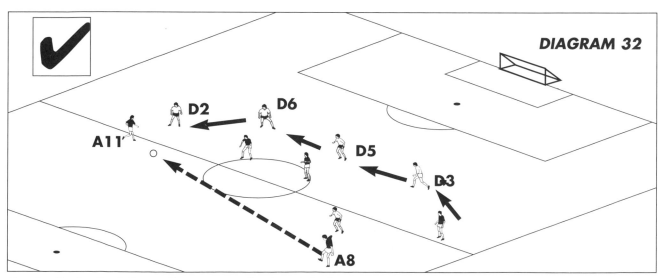

Good collective Back Four adjustment as play is switched.

A — Attacking Player   D — Defending Player

Now, **D2** is the number one player pressuring the ball. **D6** becomes the covering player. **D5**, and particularly **D3**, become balancing players.

THE MARKING TRIANGLE

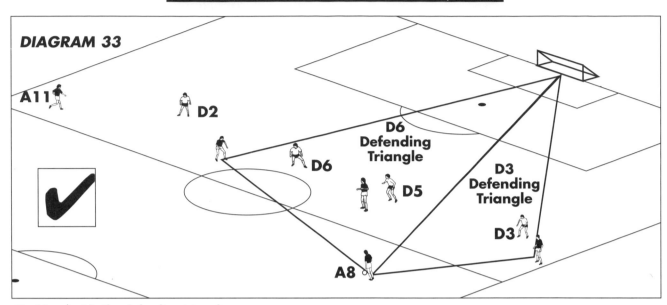

Marking inside the defending triangle.

It is wise on most occasions for the defender to be inside the marking triangle. This triangle is the one formed by drawing a line from the ball to the center of the goal, from the center of the goal to the defender's opponent, and from the opponent to the ball (Diagram 33).

D3 is in the **D3** "defending" triangle. If **D3** goes outside that triangle to the left, **D3**'s defensive position deteriorates considerably. Similarly, if **D6**'s position is 5 yards to the right and outside that defending triangle, **D6**'s position is poor. In Diagram 33, **D6**'s position is good.

Note how **D6**'s triangle changes as the ball is transferred to **A11** (Diagram 34) and how **D6** changes position because of it.

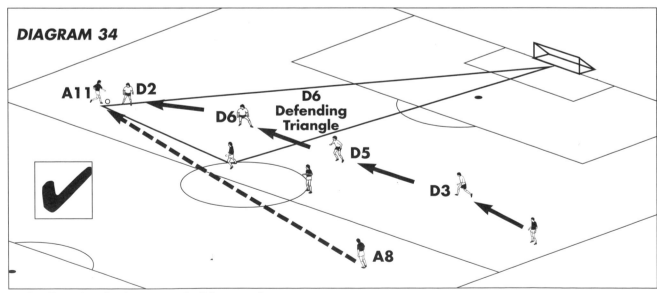

Defending triangle changes as ball is moved.

A — Attacking Player   D — Defending Player

If **D6** does not change marking position relative to **A10**, then **D6** offers **A10** the use of dangerous and advantageous space and the very good chance of **A10** being first to any pass played into this space (Diagram 35).

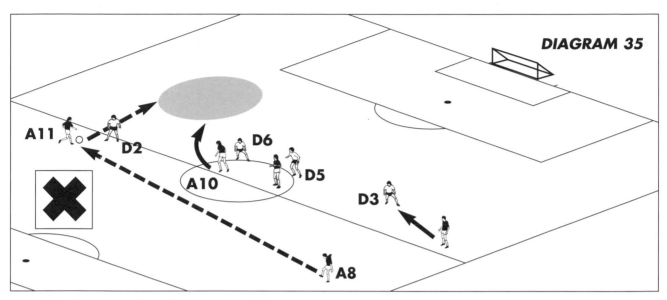

One defender's poor play places team at risk.

Marking positions therefore, in a zonal system, fulfill the main purposes, as seen from the diagrams in this section:

1) To allow a player to undertake the job of the number one defender, i.e., intercept, tackle, or challenge the ball on the attacker with the ball.

2) For the others, to occupy important space and to encourage attackers to play into less important and therefore less dangerous space.

A Short-Lived Flat Back Four!

In the early '60s, the revolution — in terms of team formations — eventually permeated down to semi-pro soccer. Initially, the outcome was hilarious.

Our fearsome manager/coach announced one day that we would start today by playing a 4-2-4!

He announced the team and was perplexed

to find he had FIVE players in his Back Four.

Some brave player had the temerity to inform the "boss" that he had included the goalkeeper in the back "four." This produced total confusion and we were curtly told to "revert to normal" — which we did. We then went on to win the league.

So much for team formations!

A — Attacking Player   D — Defending Player

CHAPTER SEVEN

The Flat Back Four — Or Is It?

There is a misconception, especially among young players and some (usually inexperienced) coaches that playing with what is known as a Flat Back Four is a euphemism for playing offside.

Firstly, I do not advocate or call it a Flat Back Four. It is, in reality, a "slightly-crooked" Back Four.

Furthermore, to play offside tactics at any level from World Cup to U12 soccer is a risky business. However, if attacking players make silly or naive early runs through the defense and run into silly and naive offside positions, it is not the job of the Back Four to run with them and keep them onside.

Furthermore, the Back Four will flatten out when it reaches the area near the penalty box. But so does any proper defensive set-up (man marking/sweeper, whatever). You cannot give deep cover in the penalty box.

But in other areas of the field, the Back Four does afford cover and, therefore, is rarely completely flat (Diagram 36).

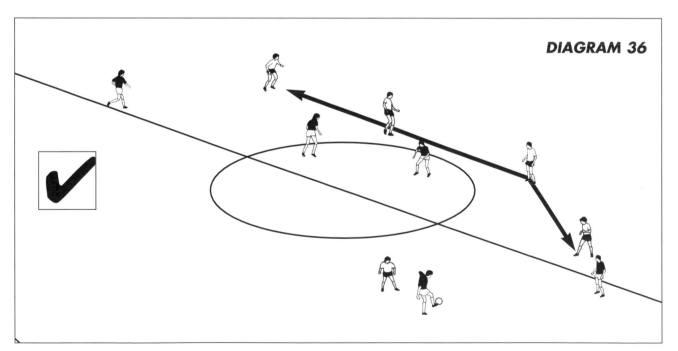

DIAGRAM 36

Wide player pressured with covering, balancing players 'flat.'

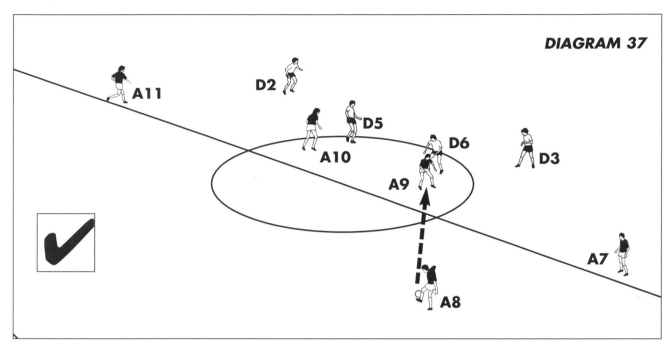

DIAGRAM 37

Central defenders "push in"...wide defenders balance.

If the ball is played to **A9**, the Back Four assumes another shape, but does offer cover (Diagram 37).

To stress it again, if the reader will forgive me, the positions taken up by **D2** and **D3** — some 5 to 6 yards behind **D5** and **D6** and tucked in — will encourage **A9** to play to **A7** or **A11**. That is across and in front of the defense. Were they to remain FLAT (Diagram 38), this would encourage **A9** and **A10** to combine with a one-two and beat **D5** and **D6**, or take them on individually.

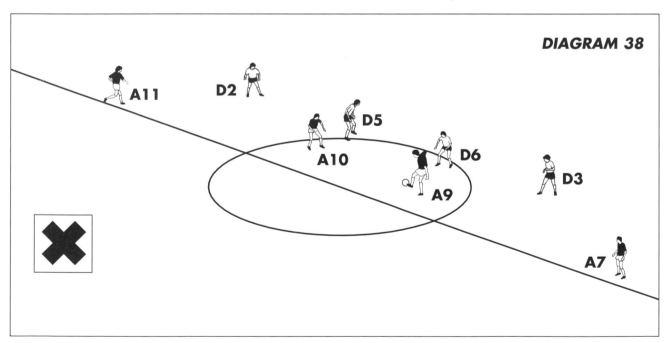

DIAGRAM 38

A "too flat" Back Four.

A — Attacking Player   D — Defending Player

Having said all that, this work and these thoughts are directed towards youth players 12- to 18-year-olds. Some professional teams and international teams play flatter than others, because of the individuals that comprise the defense. They do this because they are exceptional defenders in terms of reading the game and exceptional defenders in terms of their mental and physical speed.

Tony Waiters quoted Allan Brown in his introduction to this book: "There are many ways up Everest!" He is absolutely right. It just happens that some ways up Everest have proven to be better than others.

SOCCER — A GAME OF OPINIONS

The wonderful thing about this great game of ours is there is no ONE way of doing anything. There are fundamentals and principles — but it truly is a game of opinions.

In Zonal Defending, what should be the angle and distance of support? Where should the balancing player go? Nothing can be totally precise because, in soccer, no two situations are ever exactly the same. Inches or a foot one way or the other could be the difference.

So if you have an opinion about this book we'd like to hear it. Do you agree with what is presented? Are there some other areas you would like to have seen included?

We can always add to the book in future editions.

Dear Jack Detchon and World of Soccer...

_____

_____

_____

_____

_____

_____

Mail, fax or e-mail us at World of Soccer Inc.:

 **WORLD of SOCCER**

PO Box 3628
399 H Street, Suite 3C
Blaine WA 98231-3628

Fax: (360) 332-6078

E-mail: wos@mortimer.com

APPENDIX

BRAZIL

Carlos Alberto Pareira, the coach of Brazil at the 1994 World Cup, said on several occasions that his team played in a 4-4-2 formation. Such was the fluidity (one of the reasons for their success) that this was sometimes difficult to recognize. Pareira said that they played with a Back Four of:

Leonardo or Branco   Mario Santos   Alder   Jorginho

However, many times both flank defenders would "push up" into midfield, leaving on occasions Mario Santos and Alder to play a 2 vs 2, a situation with which the players and the coach were quite happy. At other times this "back two" would be augmented by Mauro Silva acting as a third defender.

Although Brazil does not adopt exactly the covering and marking positions shown in the principles of Zonal Defending, they were in fact responsible for zones and, to varying degrees, employed the formations they needed to play against different teams. Good players and good teams (because they are good) will adapt formations using their individual strengths and to cope with the strengths and weaknesses of different teams.

This booklet is designed to be used by coaches of young players who are trying to learn the principles of Zonal Defending — when to mark players and when to mark important space. Good teams at adult level, while adhering to the principles, will on many occasions employ players in different ways to achieve success. Our objective is to educate young players in such a way that eventually they can do just that.

I am indebted to Jerry Smith, Head Women's Soccer Coach at the University of Santa Clara, California, for his considerable insight with regard to the way Brazil plays. Jerry was with the Brazilian team throughout the '94 World Cup as a scout, coach and confidante.

PLAYERS FOR SYSTEMS?
OR SYSTEMS FOR PLAYERS?

When I took up the coaching position at Kenyon College, an outstanding All-American central defender, Leigh Sillery, was no longer available. The previous coach, Fran O'Leary, had built a formidable Zonal Defense around this Irish Youth International. Not only did Leigh understand the intricacies of playing in a Back Four, he was a terrific leader who (a) inspired players, and (b) organized, coerced and led the Back Four.

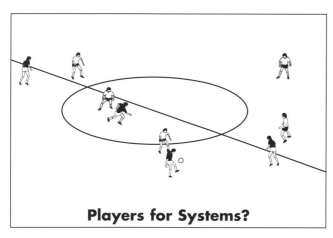

Players for Systems?

At Kenyon in 1994, none of the available defenders was happy playing in a Zonal Defense. As a result, we decided to play with 2 or 3 marking backs and a sweeper.

The players were happy with this (16 goals conceded in 37 games) because that is what they learned as young players. The pre-season training available to NCAA Division III colleges is about 10 to 12 days, which is obviously not enough time to change the habits of the players.

Since then, we have recruited 3 young men who can play zonally. Two have played that way since childhood and the third is a very gifted player ...and a quick learner.

The point of this story, then, is really two-fold (1) change the system to suit the players rather than vica-versa, and (2) utilize players in both zonal and man-for-man defenses with a sweeper, so they can become all-round players. The later in life one tries to learn something new, the more difficult (though not impossible) it becomes. Imagine learning to ride a bike at 65!!

Coaches can — and will — convert players to Zonal Defending at advanced ages, e.g., 18 to 22 and older, but it is easier to do at the age of 12.

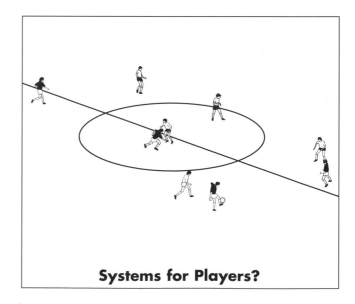

Systems for Players?

Remember, no defensive system can be successful with players who cannot mark, support, challenge and tackle. In the same way, no attacking system can succeed with players who cannot pass, control, support and shoot.

OFFSIDE

Although "Offside" is not a principle of team play, the Offside Law (Law 11) is perhaps the most important and far-reaching one in terms of team play and team strategy.

It is essential for coaches to have a full knowledge of the offside rule, its interpretation and its implementation. In the booklet "Teaching Offside," former USSF National Referee Instructor Bob Evans and Coach Tony Waiters have examined the law, its interpretation, how it should be taught to players and its tactical application.

If you are not absolutely sure of the complexities of offside, we strongly recommend reading the booklet or acquiring other manuals containing this essential information.

The fact is the referee and the linesman have total responsibility for applying the offside rule. Coaches who base their team strategy on the decisions of people outside their own organization (i.e., the referee and linesmen) will soon find themselves in trouble.

If taken advantage of, the offside rule does offer some protection to teams and does assist in developing supporting play.

The protection offered by the offside encourages the best teams of the world to push up in support of play in the attacking half, and to hold the back line of defenders for a carefully-calculated period of time in a "square" supporting position when the opposition has the ball.

This is perhaps the only situation in soccer where support is deliberately held "square" — and this tactic is not without risks. The play requires first-class understanding by teammates and the knowledge that a referee may or may not call offside — even when the players think the referee should. The referee alone makes the offside call, with or without the assistance of his linesmen. It won't do much good to dispute that decision after the fact. It will be too late.

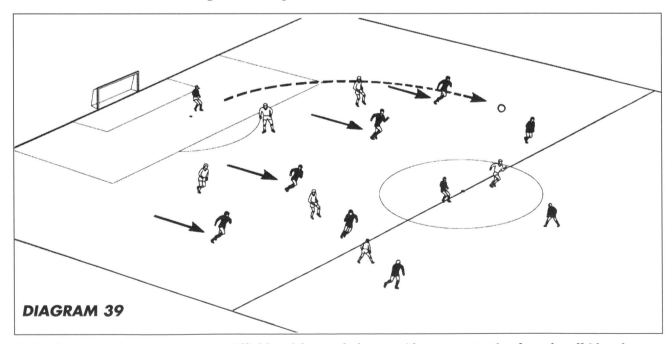

DIAGRAM 39

Back players moving out to support midfield and forward players with some protection from the offside rule

A — Attacking Player   D — Defending Player

Every good team in the world takes advantage of the offside rule to make a more effective defense. Most teams move out of deep defending positions once the ball has been cleared, but generally do not rush out helter-skelter to catch the opposition offside. They will move out to keep contact among back players, midfield and front players to maintain team "shape" and good support. They will move out to a position where they feel "comfortable." Obviously, this is sophisticated defense requiring good understanding and judgment and can only be established through coaching, practice and first-class implementation by the team.

DIAGRAM 40

Team holding a square back line until the last second.

The discipline and understanding to hold the back line in what has to be a "square" position and take advantage of the "offside" requires excellent team play. It takes fine judgment to know at what point to fall back to counter forward runs. In situations where the team "thought" a player was caught offside, there is no point in appealing to the referee for a decision while the opponent or opponents run towards the goal with the ball.

So to be successful, the team holds its position for as long as possible. If an opponent goes forward too early, he would be clearly offside. In "fine judgment" situations, nothing can be left to chance — or the referee and linesmen. Defenders must continue to play, in all circumstances retreating and tracking back. Then, an offside call is a bonus.

At Liverpool Football Club in the '70s, the coaches would say: "We never play 'offside' at Liverpool (i.e., the offside trap) but we don't stop the opposition going 'offside'." Everything in the tactical use of offside in defense comes into play in that simple statement. While the Liverpool team would play its own game, this is also a team that would only play to the whistle. Liverpool players assumed nothing while attempting to take tactical advantage of the offside rule.

For instance, a Liverpool defender would track an opponent who was going into an offside position while still allowing the attacker to be offside — but stay close enough to be able to challenge the opponent if there was no whistle.

A — Attacking Player   D — Defending Player

The Numbers Game

Objective

A fun game to encourage responsible, disciplined and skillful 1-vs-1 defending.

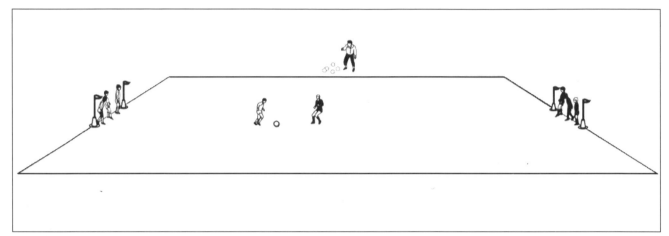

Organization

- Use a 30x20-yard Micro Soccer field.

- All players start on goal line.

- Each player on each team is given a corresponding number, e.g., 1 to 4.

- Coach calls out number e.g., "Three" and rolls the ball into play.

- The two opposing players with that number leave their goal line quickly and compete against one another.

- Coach keeps supply of balls in case one is kicked out early.

- Don't compete 1 vs 1 for longer than 20 seconds.

- Coach can call out a second number to make it 2 vs 2.

- Line players defend goal from inside 1 yard of goal line.

- Hands cannot be used.

- Ball can be played back to goalkeepers who must one-touch it back.

- Goals only count below knee height.

Coaching Points

- Defenders should close down quickly.

- Do not "dive in" to the challenge.

- Stay on the feet rather than slide-tackling.

- Defenders to chase back even when beaten.

- Angle attacker away from the center area.

Micro Soccer

Objectives

A fun 3-vs-3 game where great emphasis is placed on the attacking and defending triangles.

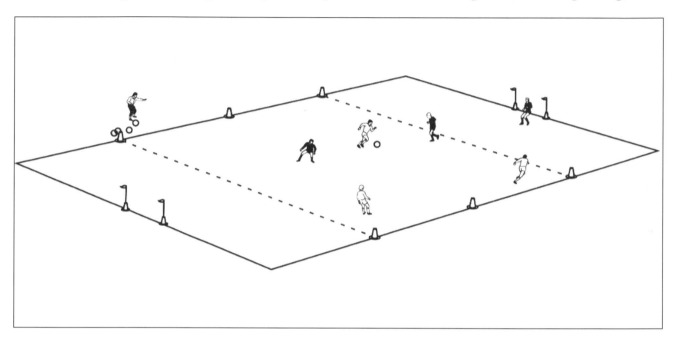

Organization

- Mark out field 20 yards x 30 yards.

- With marker disks put in 6-yard "goal boxes" for designated keeper.

- Players are rotated every 2-3 minutes so each player goes in goal.

- When ball goes out of play, game is re-started by pass-in.

- When goal is scored, re-start with goal kick.

- In practice with large numbers, have two Micro Soccer games.

- There is no offside.

- 5-yard rule at corners, kick-ins, free kicks.

Coaching Points

- Encourage first defender to go to the ball.

- The "goalkeeper" will become the rear supporting defender because of hands advantage.

- Goalkeeper needs to play a disciplined controlled "rear-defender role."

- Take away the goalkeeper role for part of the game, so that pressurizing and angle, as well as distance of supporting players, becomes even more critical.

Super 7's

Objective

A fast-changing development game having most of the critical decision-making ingredients of 11-a-side play — including offside.

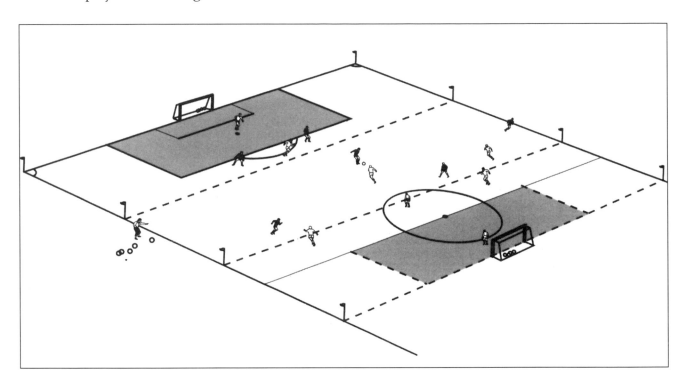

Organization

- Two teams of seven, including keepers.

- Mark line 18 yards beyond center line. Put in regulation-sized portable goal or use corner flags.

- Mark in two 25-yard lines.

- Use assistant coaches/parents as linesmen.

- Normal rules of soccer, except offside only beyond attacking 25-yard lines.

- Narrow field by 5 to 10 yards — if regulation width (i.e., 75 yards).

Coaching Points

- Be alert for the constantly-changing transitional play.

- Defensive organization to "utilize" offside.

- Encourage "total soccer" with players moving with no set positions — playing "both ways."

- Good communication.

- Encourage awareness and principles of Zonal Defending.

Three-Zone Game

A test for defenders, in zones without ball,
in marking space to give best chance of interception

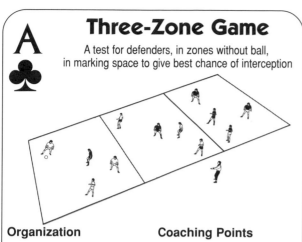

Organization

- Mark three 10x15-yd. boxes
- Split group into four teams of three identified by bibs
- 3 vs 1 in each zone
- Start at one end; possession must be retained in starting zone for at least two passes before playing to one of three players in adjacent zone
- Sequence is repeated
- Team responsible for breakdown (coach is judge!) changes with the defenders
- Coach adjusts numbers if smaller or greater than 12

Coaching Points

- Second defender must communicate with first defender.
- Second defender positions according to the good/bad defending of first defender.
- When play is in end zone, third defender acts as the "eyes" for the second defender and communicates.

Zone Game

3-vs-3 game to develop well-organized and
well-balanced defensive play

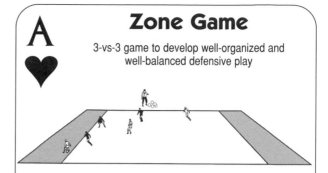

Organization

- Mark an area 30x20 yds. with additional 5-yard end zones
- "Goal" scored by dribbling or passing into end zone with ball "touched down" by sole of foot
- 3 vs 3 — with substitutes
- If ball goes out of play on sidelines re-start with kick-in (5-yard rule)
- When ball goes over end line, start in end zone of the team that did not touch it last
- One player re-starts in end zone, can pass or dribble in
- Ball live once out of endzone
- Disallow slide tackling (injuries)

Coaching Points

- First defender will determine the position of support of the other two defenders
- Important players are not "blindsided"
- When play is on one side, third defender must balance
- Quick repositioning needed when ball is passed
- Good support and "blindside" running should be promoted
- Good "collective" defending is essential
- Zonal marking should be encouraged

Chip 'n Dale

A game to test fully 3-vs-3 Zonal Defending

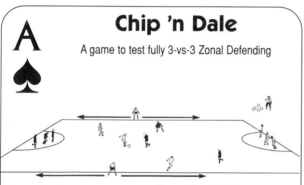

Organization

- Mark out area 35x25 yards
- Mark 1/2 circle zone at ends
- 3 vs 3 with team in possession attempting to chip ball forward into hands of teammates in zone
- To score, ball cannot bounce before reaching zone
- Ball must be caught by player in zone without catcher stepping outside
- Coach serves in balls and changes the players from the zone to the field every 3-4 mins.
- Outside players or goalkeepers are neutral and available for one-two back to team in possession

Coaching Points

- First defender must close down player with the ball
- Second defender(s) must ensure they are in correct supporting positions
- Defenders must quickly adjust when pass is made
- First defender must not "dive in" to challenge
- Third defender must balance when play is wide
- All defenders must ensure they are not "blindsided"

5 vs 3

To develop good defensive supporting play

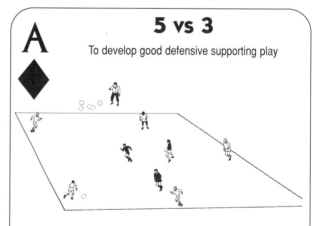

Organization

- Set up 20x20 yard areas
- 5 vs 3 in square — with 2 defenders resting
- Five attackers attempt to play five consecutive passes
- Score a goal if they do so
- Resting and active defenders changed periodically
- After 6 attempts defending, group becomes attackers and vice-versa

Coaching Points

- Defenders must combine to increase chances of "winning the ball"
- First defender can channel direction of pass
- Good communication from supporting players
- Triangular and Zonal Defending essential with attack overloaded

The Goalkeeper's Team Role

The goalkeeper is a very important member of the team — and particularly the defense. Coaches cannot ignore the goalkeepers. If they do so it is at the peril of the team — and themselves.

The goalkeeper plays an important tactical team role by being the "eyes" of the Back Four.

The goalkeeper should be encouraged to play a leadership role in communicating information to the team.

The goalkeeper should physically move up and back with the team as the ball moves up and down the field.

Of course, the goalkeeper would not normally move out much further than the edge of the penalty box.

But by "ebbing and flowing" with the team, the goalkeeper stays in contact with the field players and is better able to run out of the penalty area to clear a long "kick-and-hope" ball.

The coach must work with both the goalkeeper and the field players in certain key areas, where the goalkeeper's role assumes critical importance in the deployment of players.

These "critical areas" are:

1. **Defending at corners**

2. **Defending at free kicks**

3. **Defending at throw-ins**

4. **Moving players out of defending positions after a clearance**

5. **Instructing defenders regarding their positions, plus any adjustments required as the opposition builds an attack**

6. **Informing teammates of the goalkeeper's intended actions…e.g., coming out for a crossed ball or a through ball**

Team goalkeeping must be an integral part of all collective defending and attacking practice.

When It's Good To Have A "Big Head!"

When Bob Paisley, manager/coach of Liverpool Football Club, signed fullback Phil Neal from Third Division Northampton Town, there were many doubters. One pundit said to Paisley: "How's he going to play in the top division? He's not quick enough!"

"Oh, yeah?" said Paisley. "The first 10 yards are in his head!"

Fifty England appearances — as well as many championship medals later — Neal proved that Paisley was absolutely right.

GLOSSARY

4-4-2: A system of play that developed in the '60s based on a Zonal Back Four with four midfield players and two front runners. It was considered a more defensive arrangement than the 4-2-4 formation that preceded it.

BACK FOUR: Comprises a right outside defender (fullback), a left outside defender (left fullback) and two central defenders, usually playing left and right central. Nowadays, a Back Four is used more generically to mean a way of playing a zonal system even if in reality it is a Back Three (even a Back Two) rather than a Back Four.

BALANCE: The positioning of "Third Defenders" or "Distant Support" that gives team collective "shape" and effectiveness.

BALL WATCHERS: Players when defending who become preoccupied in seeing where the ball is and by doing so lose sight of key opponent(s).

COVER: See "Support."

FLAT BACK FOUR: See Back Four. This is where not only traditional positions and zones are observed but also where the back players take advantage of the offside law to play square or flat.

MAN-FOR-MAN MARKING: Where a player (or players) is (are) assigned an opponent to mark. The extent to which this is done at the exclusion of all other considerations depends on the system and the coach. Man-for-man marking is a generic soccer term respective of gender and will probably remain so because of ease of communication, e.g., "Mark your man!" is more economic and definitive than "Mark your player!"

PASSING ON (see Tracking): Where a marking player, usually by instruction from another teammate, allows the immediate opponent to make a run without being "tracked"— with another teammate picking up the player when he/she moves into the teammate's zone.

PUSH UP (or Push In): Where back, midfield and front players move forward collectively to constrict the space of the team in possession. It has a reliance on the offside law for its effectiveness.

SERVER: The person (coach or player) who starts the practice by "serving" the ball in — usually by passing.

SLIDING: The movement of covering and supporting back players where, instead of moving into a full supporting position by running on a direct route back towards the goal, they move inside to take some advantage of the protection of offside.

SPACE MARKING: Like Zonal Defending, where the player is as concerned about marking dangerous space as marking an attacker.

SQUARE DEFENSE: In Zonal Defending, where the back players hold a flat position to take advantage of the offside law.

SUPPORT: The help given to the player on the ball (attack) or pressurizing the player with the ball (defense). There are two kinds of defensive support: (1) Near — which normally means the teammate who is immediately behind the player nearest to the ball; (2) Distant — player or players who are giving depth and balance to the defensive organization.

SWEEPER: A player with no specific man-marking responsibilities, who usually plays behind the man-marking rear defenders to give cover. Normally, this person is an intelligent player who reads the game especially well.

TRACKING: Moving and staying with an opponent who has made a run forwards, sideways, backwards or diagonally when there is no opportunity of "passing on" the player for another teammate to assume the marking responsibility.

TARGET PLAYER: In a practice, the player who will receive the ball to complete the exercise successfully.

ZONAL DEFENDING — Where the defense is as much concerned about marking dangerous space as marking players.

NOTES